JUSTICE SERIES - VOL 4

THE WAY OF JUSTICE

THE GAME CHANGER

STEFFRON T. JAMES

THE WAY OF JUSTICE

ISBN: 978-0-9998144-8-2
ISBN: 978-0-9998144-9-9 (eBook)

Copyright © 2020 by The Way of Justice - All Rights Reserved.
THE WAY OF JUSTICE: *The Game Changer*
By Steffron T. James

Unless otherwise indicated, all Scripture quotations are from The ESV® Bible (The Holy Bible, English Standard Version®), copyright © 2001 by Crossway, a publishing ministry of Good News Publishers. Used by permission. All rights reserved.

All rights reserved under International Copyright Law. Except as permitted under the U.S. Copyright Act of 1976, no part of this publication may be reproduced, distributed, or transmitted in any form or by any means, or stored in a database or retrieval system, without the prior written permission of the publisher.

Editor: Tosha Jones of JMC Marketing & Communications (tjones@thejmc.com)
Nashville, Tennessee USA

Content Editor: Debra D. Winans of Linking Solutions LLC (linkingdolutions.net)
Atlanta, Georgia USA

Design & Layout: Michael Matulka of Basik Studios (www.gobasik.com)
Omaha, Nebraska USA

Publisher: Kingdom Living Ministries - Publishing (www.thewayofjustice.com)
Murfreesboro, Tennessee USA

Printed in the United States of America

10 9 8 7 6 5 4 3 2 1

"THE RIGHTEOUS WAY IS THE WAY OF JUSTICE"

- Steffron T. James

PREFACE
A FRESH PERSPECTIVE ON JUSTICE

In this booklet, *The Way of Justice*, we will discuss how true justice can help people navigate their way through difficult and tragic situations; we will learn about the correlation between love and justice; we will examine the lives of legendary Bible characters whose just actions paved a way and an example for the people who followed their leadership; and we'll consider how every person can make a difference in someone else's life if he or she is committed to acting in a righteous and just way every day.

> *[7] "The path of life is level for those who are right with God; LORD, you make the way of life smooth for those people. [8] But, LORD, we are waiting for your way of justice. Our souls want to remember you and your name. [9] My soul wants to be with you at night, and my spirit wants to be with you at the dawn of every day. When your way of justice comes to the land, people of the world will learn the right way of living."*
>
> *- Isaiah 26:7-9 (NCV)*

Although I am starting this section of the introduction with a scripture, my heart's desire is to write in a way that encourages believers, non-believers, spiritual, non-spiritual, churched, un-churched, agnostic, or atheist to be able to read my books and find information that will assist them in living life more effectively. When I explore the topic of justice, I am acutely aware justice is not a Christian-exclusive need. Justice is actually a foundational pillar for all humanity. When we relegate justice to that which we employ only after heinous acts, atrocities, or what we deem unjust actions, then we short-circuit the true justice intent. Justice has to be integrated into personal daily aspirations. I feel we totally miss its necessity and its nature when we operate otherwise. No matter who you are, justice can calibrate the effectiveness of your world.

Justice is a living and breathing way to approach life so that as you collide with unforeseen, unanticipated, unpredictable, and prodigious encounters, your behaviors, thoughts, responses, emotions, direction, and mode of operation can be easily measured by your own personal self-assessment (PSA) or, should the need arise, assessment from without. Justice is a healthy objective measure for balance in an imbalanced world.

We often hear individuals say, "don't judge me." Well, my question is why don't you invite judgment? None of us come to the earth perfect. If you are not judged, then how do you get better? How do we change that which is negative, toxic, harmful, unproductive, stagnant, and counter to us? How do we find our best if we are not willing to do our own PSA or invite external evaluation, judgment?

I know, people can be cruel. However, you have to learn to deal with the cruel while discerning whose evaluation is valid. Even a negative evaluation from a negative person can be extremely enlightening. Every company, organization, institution, and even governments are continuously evaluating their effectiveness. They do what is now called SWOT analysis (Strengths-Weaknesses-Opportunities-Threats).

During my years serving in the military, being in business, pastoring, mentoring, training, and teaching, I've learned that which is not willing to be judged never improves.

We can call it whatever makes us feel warm and fuzzy inside, but the bottom line is if we desire to do life better, if we desire to be effective in life, if we want who we are as individuals to count and have value, then the perspectives of people around us is one of our best tools of improvement (whether we enjoy it, like it, hate it or not). So, it would behoove us to start welcoming and inviting any input that can positively shape us into who we want to be as individual people.

Essential for all is the understanding we need shaping as friends, brothers, sisters, mothers, fathers, cousins, wives, husbands, children, orphans, abused, oppressed, fired, hired, students, elderly, handicap, diagnosed with a disease, and a person who just won a million dollars. Any of these areas and thousands more require a wide-eyed understanding that life happens to all.

INTRODUCTION

A desire. A thirst. A longing for significance. These are the catalysts that have compelled me to write a four-part series about the concept of justice.

Over the past four years, I have been taken to school and to task on this subject that I didn't know had relevance to my purpose or destiny in life. I am a believer in God, but this subject is not limited to, nor exclusive to those of like mind. It is a societal issue and need.

I have discovered that justice may be one of the most misunderstood, but beneficial concepts known to man. However, it may possess the opportunity to right many of the ill we face with humanity. Understanding justice and applying its principles can change governments, countries, cities, individuals, and all in between. It is a way to approach life, other people, situations, and circumstances with balance and soundness.

I know what you are thinking; I must be selling some magic pill or potion. I assure you; I was as shocked as any when I began to realize the implications of this subject. I was even more shocked with the overwhelmingly positive responses I got as I began to share it with others. Individuals who I respect and know to be more studious, well-informed, well-read, contemplative, and honestly smarter than me encouraged me to write this four-part series.

My first book, *Champions of Justice*, was very in-depth and technical. The feedback I received was to present the same information in smaller, bite-sized pieces that are easier to digest and embrace. This would allow those who are newly introduced to the concept of justice to truly grasp its implications and understand its impact.

You are about to eat a small meal that will hopefully keep bringing you back to the table. If you want the full-course meal all at once, you can order *Champions of Justice* from our website: *www.thewayofjustice.com*.

I pray the reading of each book (The Cause of Justice, The Streets of Justice, The Path of Justice, and The Way of Justice) will expose you little-by-little to the relevance and necessity of understanding the concept of justice. These books truly give us a culture-changing perspective of justice.

ENJOY THE APPETIZER!

TABLE OF CONTENT

Preface: A Fresh Perspective on Justice iii

Introduction v

Chapter One: Triumphant Tragedy 1

Chapter Two: What's love got to do with it? 5

Chapter Three: Your Moment 9

Chapter Four: Anywhere, Really? 13

Chapter Five: "The Way" 19

About the Author 35

Other Books Available 36

THE WAY OF JUSTICE

STEFFRON T. JAMES

CHAPTER ONE
TRIUMPHANT TRAGEDY

No one is exempt from tragedy, disappointment, betrayal, elation, frustration, fear, or fantasy. However, not knowing how to face or navigate any of these events can derail the best of us. We must have mooring straps, anchors, tent pins, and guiding lights for dark times where nothing can be seen clearly or understood. There are times our worlds are turned up-side-down leaving us devoid of any direction. It will take a force, an unwavering conviction, a principle so strong it even trumps tragedy to bring us to a semblance of normalcy when nothing seems normal. It will be the light that takes you by the hand and leads you to a place of fulfillment, purpose, and usefulness.

It would be great to have a person in our life at the perfect time to guide us at the exact moment of our greatest need. That would be ideal. I know you say, "but God, but Jesus, but the Holy Spirit is there." I get that, and I believe they are also. However, when the proverbial "it" happens to you, it's hard to see God, especially if blaming Him is one of your coping mechanisms, as a means of directing your anger so you don't burst from the inside. Having a person who gets you and knows how to walk you through what you have never faced is usually not possible without a great deal of front-end preparation for you and the person. More times than not, most never take the opportunity to establish or don't even consider such things.

I have found in my fifty-seven years of being on the earth, the situations that have potential to wreck my world are not the situations, but the lack of preparation for the situations I know can wreck my world. We don't consider the worst-case scenarios, so when it happens, it devastates us.

A newly married couple loses their first child. A single mom loses her job. You are diagnosed with a life-threatening decease. Your wife leaves you for your best friend. Someone you love is killed in a car accident. News radio, television, internet, and vocal person in the office remind us of the indiscriminate nature of tragedy. Recently, I was traveling on Interstate 65 on a return trip from Montgomery Alabama heading back to Tennessee. I'd been watching my youngest daughter, who's in her senior year of college, play in her final regular season volleyball match. As I listened to music, I got a glimpse of one of those cross monuments you see on the side of the road where someone in an accident has died. This one in particular caught my attention and was quickly gone from sight, but not from my thinking. The memorial had two larger crosses and three smaller ones. My first thought was an entire family lost. Then the thought hit me! What if someone survived? What if there was one person in the immediate family not in the vehicle when the rest perished? How would that person deal with the devastation, possible guilt, the pain, and loss knowing nothing in his or her world would ever be the same again. What would grandma and grandpa experience? What would siblings and friends have to cope with? We are not exempt from the stabbing whims of life, that leave us afraid. I had to ask myself in that moment, "What if?"

These factors, do and can happen to anyone. The thing is, we are often so devastated we cease to exist as a person; yet and still, we have to navigate the plight we face. Our responses to the plight, could inflict as much or more far reaching damage to those closest to us, than the origin misfortune. Families, companies, futures and lives have been ripped apart because of one individual's lack of understanding preparation for tragedy.

Imagine you are a small business owner with twenty-five employees. You have grown the business for over fifteen years adding an average of one and a half new employees per year. You are the visionary; you are the lead; you are the inspiration that carries the entire ship forward. But tragedy hits you unexpectedly. You lose your wife and only child in a fire. I know that is unthinkable, but it does happen. I am not being morbid, I promise. But if I don't say these things, then you will not be ready. For the next year, you are numb, nothing makes sense. You question your purpose. Your constant question is, "why does any of it really matter?" Everyone around you is empathetic, loving, supportive, and encouraging; but those at your business with families, homes, mortgages, responsibilities are seeing previous clients now leave and the business is faltering. What are they to do? Is it insensitive to approach you? Are they being judgmental to ask how you're handling your grief? What is actually off limits? What are the boundaries? Are there any answers? God help us all!

I've been doing an intense study about justice for the past few years. When I originally came across this term, I felt it was another tool I could hook to my proverbial tool belt to use if the need arose. However, over the last year or so, I have had an awakening and come to discover it is not only a tool, but one of those multi-functional gadgets that can be a help in the most tragic situations. I know, you are skeptical. But let me explain before I give the term, even though you may know what it is from the opening passage. When we face uncertainty, pain, confusion, loss, or tragedy, oftentimes we are at a loss for what to do. We don't know if we should be angry, cry, mourn, laugh, sing, shout, scream, hit something, or just die ourselves. But if you had a "default what" in every situation, would that help you? Before I tell you the word, the concept. Let me tell you a story I heard over twenty years ago. Until now, I had no idea about its relevance.

A woman living in Alaska had two beautiful twin daughters. They were 11 years old. The mother had lost her husband to illness years earlier. But she had her girls and they gave her great joy. On Thanksgiving Day while traveling back home from dinner with friends, the woman lost control of her vehicle and had a terrible accident. One of the twins was pronounced dead at the scene of the accident. The other was rushed to the hospital in critical condition. The second twin lived until Christmas day, then she also died. The mother was devastated to say the least.

But, the lady was a believer in God and here is what she communicated to those who came to console her. "I loved my girls with everything within me. I will miss them terribly. But God allowed me to have the gift of them, the joy of them for eleven years. I thank Him for that. I am not sure all of His plans for my life, but I will not let the love I had for my daughters go to waste."

THE WAY OF JUSTICE

A short time later, the woman started taking in young girls without parents. Eventually she opened an orphanage to assist young displaced girls, and she became their mother. This lady did what I am talking about; she responded to tragedy and loss with actions that turn things good for others first, then for the person with the right response.

Many have launched out of the ashes of tragedies and have ventured into areas of support, help, advocacy, righting of wrongs, and correcting injustice because of an uninvited plight suffered at the hands of life. Mothers, fathers, brothers, sisters, friends, and those we might not know are heroes, willingly using their capabilities and means to put things right for others, in spite of the darkness they endured. Is it noble? Is it honorable? Is it commendable? My answer is a resounding, "yes!" I truly believe God never wastes a hurt; as a matter of fact, he wastes nothing at all. But we have to get past our hurt to see our purpose in the pain, and His purpose in and through our devastation.

We often ask why did something so horrible occur? I would imagine in the midst of that mother losing her children, she asked many questions quietly within herself. Yet, in the midst of her devastation, a few questions began to elevate above others.

1. What is the purpose of this?

2. What will my life look like now?

3. What's my new normal?

The answer may have not been immediately evident. But that mother quickly chose to trust the God of her daughters that entrusted her with the privilege of two wonderful gifts for eleven years. The intent of our lives does not die or end even with those we love immeasurably, though it may feel that way. Often our story begins at the end of tragedy. Our way is not revealed until we can no longer see which way to go. Many times, it is not the start of our story nor the end, but the paths, the ways and the directions we choose that were seemingly insignificant in the moment. But we can point back to a conscious thing we chose.

Here is what I am saying, I believe we can prepare for that choice. It doesn't have to be haphazard in the moment. Else, years later you are pondering regrets and disappointments for a choice not measured by any meaningful standard.

I included Isaiah 26:7-9 in the beginning of this book.

> [7] "The path of life is level for those who are right with God; LORD, you make the way of life smooth for those people. [8] But, LORD, we are waiting for your way of justice. Our souls want to remember you and your name. [9] My soul wants to be with you at night, and my spirit wants to be with you at the dawn of every day. When your way of justice comes to the land, people of the world will learn the right way of living."
>
> - Isaiah 26:7-9 (NCV)

When I read this scripture for the first time, I honestly was unsure if I could accept or appreciate what it was saying. I knew it carried some tremendous insight and seemed to be a trump card, solution, inspiration, a guide, an illumination of a possible "anytime direction" to take. However, I am a skeptic of anything that becomes the key, the only, the one thing, the end all be all for life. Let me tell you why I say that. I've heard the messages, "all you have to have is love," "all you have to have is faith," "all you have to have is grace," "all you have to have is the Word," "and all you have to have is the Holy Spirit." There are probably others, but you get my point.

Here is the quandary, I get why these statements are made, because in given situations they are what has been the answer in the stories of countless thousands. But just as they were the answers for thousands, they provided no comfort or answers for multitudes of others. Love is a must have. But it is often hard to quantify. Love is why we do much of what we do, but doesn't often give us what to do. Grace is vitally necessary, but knowing grace has provided all I will ever need doesn't tell me *how* to navigate the treachery I currently face. The Word is more powerful than anything anyone can imagine and though it is the place any can turn for comfort, instruction, wisdom, and insight; knowing *what* to apply and *when* to apply it can

THE WAY OF JUSTICE

be the difference between success and failure. This also must be taken into account, the individual would have to be well-studied and well-versed in scripture to locate the ideal, applicable, and relevant principle to engage in their situation. Remember this could be at a very dark or devastating time in life.

I would like to introduce you to justice. Justice as I see it is a light, direction, safety net, or rescue line to pull you to safety while you figure out what's next. I believe justice deliberately takes the focus off of us, pulls us into someone else's story, freeing us of ourselves. Let me explain.

Regardless of what we face, if we still have breath, we have capability and means with our thoughts, attitudes, energy, words, resources, and actions that can be the most unexpected change agents to others.

Recently there was a story that captured the national headlines. A white female police officer shot a black man when she accidentally entered the wrong apartment thinking it was hers. She killed a man who was innocent. The circumstances of the trial and investigation ended in her being found guilty of manslaughter. Before the sentencing, the brother of the deceased man (in a wonderful move of compassion and mercy) embraced the white officer and told her he forgave her and wanted nothing but good will towards her. She was still going to face jail time (justice served), but in this situation his justice was what provided her with a gracious mercy not seen or embraced by many. The brother of the deceased man took the opportunity in tragedy to lend compassion to who most would consider an undeserving recipient.

Justice provides anyone opportunity to put things right for others, by using their capability and means. Let's say you are the person who has experienced tragedy. You are dazed and confused. But the one thing you know to do is to be just. You don't know much, but you know you can willing use your capability and means to put things right for someone else. Like the mother who opened her home to be a mother to girls she didn't give birth to but loved as her own.

Justice becomes your clutch response. If you know the criteria for justice, then it will always give you the next step, the next action, the focus, the direction, the path out. Love will come; faith will come; grace will come; but the face of them all will be justice. When we bring justice to others regardless of what we feel, it penetrates the weeds allowing us to sense and embrace that which is bigger than even what we face. Justice becomes our "what" to take us to our "how and why!" Let's look back at Isaiah 26:7-9.

> [7] "The **path of life** is level for those who are right with God; LORD, you make the **way of life** smooth for those people. [8] But, LORD, we are waiting for your **way of justice**. Our souls want to remember you and your name. [9] My soul wants to be with you at night, and my spirit wants to be with you at the dawn of every day. When your way of justice comes to the land, people of the world will learn **the right way of living**."
>
> - Isaiah 26:7-9 (NCV)

Would it be okay if I started with verse eight? " But, Lord, we are waiting for your **way** of justice." Why is this so vital? Can you here the longing in the passage? Verse seven talks of two things: the path of life and the way of life. Obviously there has been terrible turbulence faced on the path of life and the way of life for the writer's audience; however, the path is considered level and the way is considered smooth. What brings about these two things? Answer: "We are waiting for your (God's) way of justice." Can I go out of order again as we break this down? The second part of verse nine, "When your way of justice comes to the land, people of the world will learn the right way of living." There is a path, there is a way being illuminated to others that will change everything. I believe justice is a game changer! We are told by the scriptures we are to be a light. What kind of light? What is our light to show? What makes each of our lights homogeneous where they are seen as the same no matter where you see them in the world? That has been the problem. There has not been a consistency in our shine. The inconsistency of shine leaves nothing for others to learn from. There is a *right way to shine!*

"JUSTICE BECOMES OUR "WHAT" TO TAKE US TO OUR "HOW AND WHY!"

THE WAY OF JUSTICE

"My soul (our mind, emotions, and intellect) wants to be with you at night, and "my spirit (the very nature and core of my being) wants (longs) to be with you at the dawn of every day."

In verse nine the writer gets personal. At the end of verse eight the statement is inclusive, "our souls want to remember you and your name." What would make them forget God's name? The difficulty of their plight. So, the writer tells them it will require making it so personal their yearning has to resonate from deep inside them.

When we have experienced the deepest loss imaginable, what can bring us out of it? What has brought back most who have returned to some semblance of a functional life after devastation?

Number one is seeing or knowing others who "willingly used their capabilities and means in a similar situation to put things right for others." Knowing others didn't focus on how wrong their circumstances were, but on what they could make level and smooth for others gave hope. We are staggered and floored when we see those who have every reason to be bitter, angry, withdrawn, isolated, curled up in a fetal position, or seeking vengeance turn their focus to helping others. Zechariah 8:16 from a combination of the ESV and NKJV says, *"these are the things you shall do, speak truth to one another, render in your gates justice that is true and makes for peace."*

"In your gates" means within your power to control and determine outcomes. Others need to learn from your life. Life is hard and hard to navigate. But there is a way that smoothes and levels even in and through the worst of times. Life happens to all; all will choose how to respond. But it is those who long to be justice advocates who will be a light.

CHAPTER TWO
WHAT'S LOVE GOT TO DO WITH IT?

"Who is my neighbor?" That was the question.

In a parable in the tenth chapter of Luke, a Samaritan man had found a person who had experienced devastation. He was robbed, beaten, and left for dead. This Samaritan found him, administered first aid, carried the injured man to a nearby town and cared for him until he began to amend. When the Samaritan departed the town, he left strict instructions for the person's care and he promised to provide additional funds for the man's care if needed

This is a neighbor that is a light! This is a just neighbor who made the way smooth and level for another. What will the injured man think? Did the Samaritan show him a way of justice? Can the injured man ever easily forget this Samaritan (who by the way was supposed to be an enemy of the man's social and cultural group)? An enemy showed the light! I suggest, when such a light is shown by an enemy, it is one of the brightest lights imaginable. The injured man learned **the right way of living** from what was thought to be an enemy!

Jesus answered the question, "who is my neighbor," with that parable. He then instructs the lawyer who asked him the question to "go do likewise."

I say to us, *before* our tragic occurrence, "do likewise;" *in* our tragic occurrence, "do likewise;" to *get out* of our tragic occurrence, "do likewise!"

If we have done likewise, perhaps that light will be shone on us in our greatest time of need. The world will learn the right way of living,

THE WAY OF JUSTICE

"likewise justice," putting things right for others in a just way for the just One. Justice becomes the reset! Justice is the recalibration to smooth and level for all that has become chaotic and turbulent. Justice makes sense out of nonsense. Justice rights wrongs with right behaviors. Justice brings order to confusion! Justice provides guidance on what to do when nothing else is known.

Why do I emphasize justice and not love? In John 13:35, Jesus said, *"by this all will know that you are my disciples, because you have love for one another."* This verse indicates people will know you have love for one another. Love is *why* we do what we do; justice gives us *what* to do! **You can't have love without justice, but you can have justice without love.**

Justice is possibly the most beautiful demonstration of love that may not have anything to do with love. You could almost say, like the lyrics of the Tina Turner song, "What's love got to do with it?" I want to ask you a question. How long does it take for mature love to happen? What do you do in the interim? Okay, it was two questions. Love is the overarching reason God gave us justice; but love may not be why we operated in justice. Justice is love without emotion! Justice is love without the need for good feelings towards another, though they are welcome and invited. The first assignment to man wasn't to love. It was be fruitful, multiply, subdue, and have dominion. Man was not put on the earth to simply live life. He was put here to have life and give life also. Those who give life live the most fulfilled lives. Jesus in the book of John indicated the greatest love and honor you can show God and the world is doing what we were created to do.

> [4] *"I glorified you on earth, having accomplished the work that you gave me to do"*
>
> - John 17:4 (ESV)

"NEVER FORGET THAT JUSTICE IS WHAT LOVE LOOKS LIKE IN PUBLIC"
- AMERICAN PHILOSOPHER CORNEL WEST.

Willingly using our capability and means to be fruitful, multiply, subdue, rule, and have dominion in order to put things right for others *is* justice. We receive places of rule to give others a chance to rule. Right rule has right motivations, intentions, responses, and behaviors that model, invite, welcome, and facilitate the rule of others. Right rule fosters an environment of maximum yield. Let me explain.

When we are our most fruitful, we produce fruit for others to enjoy. When we multiply, we create abundance for others to get portions. When we subdue, rule, and have dominion, it opens opportunities for others in the wake of our efforts. As we do our best, it pulls the best from others. Our places of mastery allow others to find mastery. We beget what we produce. Others beget what we make available. Justice is willingly making available your capability and means. Allowing justice to be fruitful, multiply, subdue, rule and have dominion in your life demonstrates love.

God understood our initial inability to love as He does, so with justice He gave us what would be the epitome, the personification, the archetype, the embodiment, the ultimate demonstration of His love until we grew up to be like Him. Let me give you an example.

You meet someone new and think they hung the moon; they are the most wonderful person ever. You quickly fall in love with that person. I am not saying it can't happen and that it doesn't at times work out. However, I see it as just a little haughty, prideful, somewhat foolish, and from a place of ignorance to say "I love you" to someone like this who you've known for only one year. You love what you know about the person so far. As you get to know the person more, you learn more about the person's flaws, shortcomings, and quirks. Then you get to *choose* to love. Could it be you are not necessarily falling in love, but falling into infatuation?

I also find it disingenuous to say to a stranger, "I love you with the love of Christ." But I hear it all the time. Do I believe love is possible for us? Absolutely. But only as much as we love God and what He loves. Justice allows time for love to materialize. Justice is the true essence of God's love for us, until the essence of our love for Him and others shows up.

JUSTICE ISN'T PASSIVE! IT IS TO BE ESTABLISHED, EXECUTED, ENFORCED, AND EXEMPLIFIED.

Justice is the default for those who would be faultless. Most justice we see is responsive. Someone commits an act or atrocity, then we go into "justice mode" saying it has to be responded to. But true justice works at having things right and putting things right as a way of life, so a corrective justice response is not required. If we judge ourselves, we will not be judged. When is judgment not allowed? Because the scripture clearly says in several places, "judge not." Judgment in the scripture is when you deem anyone unworthy of justice. Your thought process is, this person is of such little value they don't deserve my capability and means, they don't deserve my just treatment. How can you deny justice and say you love? It is impossible! A person of justice recognizes and understands that withholding justice from an individual who doesn't "deserve" justice makes himself a perpetuator of injustice and strips away the redemptive opportunity afforded by true justice. To do unjustly to the unjust, makes you unjust! Love is not acquainted with injustice. Love eradicates it!

CHAPTER THREE
YOUR MOMENT

There is a part of the justice of God that has to do with vengeance. But I want to say right from the onset, that is God's business. Here are the references!

> [30] *"For we know him who said,*
> *"Vengeance is mine; I will repay." And again,*
> *"The Lord will judge his people."*
>
> *- Hebrews 10:30 (ESV)*

> [19] *"Beloved, never avenge yourselves,*
> *but leave it to the wrath of God, for it is written,*
> *"Vengeance is mine, I will repay, says the Lord."*
>
> *- Romans 12:19 (ESV)*

We are told in Romans "never avenge yourself." It doesn't even say we can ask God to avenge us. This does not mean God will not avenge us. However, His vengeance I believe is redemptive. "Love your enemy, do good to those who persecute you, bless those who do you wrong." This is the vengeance the Lord uses to make your enemies be at peace with you. This is the power of putting things right for others. Which is the brighter light? Your actions turning a dark heart to light or seeing a dark heart crushed?

Solomon was a great King that came to power at a time when there were many who didn't celebrate His rise to the throne. He had enemies who would have loved to take him out. His father David had turned the throne over to him and it was treason for anyone to try to dethrone him. However, after a specific prayer he prays, God takes note and acknowledges because he didn't ask for the life of his enemies, it made him possibly the greatest king ever.

THE WAY OF JUSTICE

> [11] "Then God said to him, "Because you have asked this thing, and have not asked long life for yourself, nor have asked riches for yourself, nor have asked the life of your enemies, **but have asked for yourself understanding to discern justice**, [12] behold, I have done according to your words; see, I have given you a wise and understanding heart, so that there has not been anyone like you before you, nor shall any like you arise after you. [13] **And I have also given you what you have not asked: both riches and honor**, so that there shall not be anyone like you among the kings all your days."
>
> - 1Kings 3:11-13 (NJKV)

There is a great deal here. But for our purposes, let's just look at two.

"This thing" stands out as the key to this great king's success. I believe all of us will have our "this thing" moment. Besides our accepting God, His Son, and His plan for our lives, we have to decide if we want to live with Him, His way. I know we can know God, but do we know His ways, how He functions and operates?

Solomon's request was for the understanding to discern justice. This was the key to all that followed for him. He didn't ask for long life for himself, riches, nor for the life or vengeance against his enemies. Knowing justice was his request. Evil men do not understand justice, but those who seek the Lord understand it completely. (Proverbs 28:5) Do you understand justice completely? Solomon made this his number one request and he became one of the greatest kings ever. I think when we truly get justice, we finally have a chance to get God.

Let's look back at the second thing our verse from Kings shows us. "There shall not be anyone like you." What a statement! When justice is what you do, you become incomparable! You become a model for others.

History reveals kings, governments, officials, and the curious came from all over the known world to marvel at King Solomon. One of the people who came understood his genius. She saw the key! She said:

> [8] *"Blessed be the LORD your God, who has delighted in you and set you on his throne as king for the LORD your God! Because your God loved Israel and would **establish** them forever, he has made you king over them, that you may **execute justice and righteousness**."*
>
> *- 2 Chronicles 9:8 (ESV)*

This declaration came from the Queen of Sheba who was said to be quite majestic in her own rite. She attributed all that this King had accomplished to his execution of "justice and righteousness" to and for others! Whether king, teacher, janitor, cook, soldier, athlete, corporate executive, stay-at-home mom, or delivery driver; what happens when you decide your way will be the way of justice? Everything simplifies! When will you have your "this thing" moment, it prepares you for your proverbial "it." Let's look at another standout Bible personality!

Abraham, is considered one of, if not the most, notable personalities in the Bible. He is the prominent figure on which everything launches in the Old Testament for the Jewish people and the central figure as an example to model in the New Testament. He is called the father of faith and we as believers are called the spiritual seed of Abraham. Father means source. When something is the source, what's in the source flows to everything coming after it. What it flows to, gets to be a partaker and recipient of that source. So, what was the *source* leading to Abraham's greatness, to his enduring legacy in the Bible, his identification as the man of faith? What was the key to his standing out as the one whose generations would live on through the annals of history? Many were great and never heard of again, but this man far exceeded all. *"He will be heir of the world."* (Romans 4:13) This is a promise to Abraham that flows to those who are his offspring, whether naturally or spiritually. Let me give you just a bit of context.

Abraham had left his home country with his father, Terah, to go to a land that God would show them. Abraham's father never made it to the land. He stopped in a place called Haran and died there. Interestingly, Terah had a son who died earlier in his life whose name was Haran. Just a side note, "don't let the life of a loved one end your life." After Terah died, God spoke to his son Abraham and told him to proceed to a land he would be shown. Abraham went through extreme challenges with famine, peril, enemies, and the most difficult...not having a child. This difficulty was exacerbated by the fact he and his wife Sarah were getting old. But then God came to him and promised him a son. He also added that Abraham's offspring would be as numerous as the sand on the sea shore and the stars of heaven.

After that promise it was twenty-five years *before* he and his wife had a son. He was one hundred and she was over ninety years old when the child arrived. Wonderful, now they had a son. But wait; this same God asks Abraham to offer the new son in sacrifice to Him as an act of obedience and faith. Abraham believes God is able to even raise the boy from the dead, if need be, so he begins the action to slay the boy. At the last minute, an angel stops Abraham with a knife in his hand. There is a ram in a nearby bush that miraculously appears. Abraham offers the ram and the boy is spared.

Abraham is considered from that moment the "father of faith," for his selfless act and trust of God's provision. It is believed by many that "this moment" changed everything for Abraham.

I have a different theory I would like for you to consider. Was having a child at one hundred spectacular? Was his wife getting pregnant, carrying to term, and delivering a child at ninety plus a miracle? Was being willing to offer God his long-awaited son an act beyond compare? I say yes to all the above and these things should surely stand out as reasons for Abrahams notoriety! But are they the events that brought all of God's promises to Abraham?

Take a look with me at a conversation God had with Abraham the day the child was promised.

> [19] *"For I have chosen him, that he may command his children and his household after him to keep **the way of the LORD** by doing righteousness and justice, so that the **LORD** may bring to **Abraham** what he has **promised him**."*
>
> *- Genesis 18:19 (ESV)*

Why could God trust Abraham to bring him a child? Because God believes Abraham would teach his children and anyone in his household to keep the "way" of the Lord. So, what is the way of the Lord? I thought you'd never ask! Doing "righteousness and justice" is what is indicated in the text. But I want to draw attention to justice.

We have taught righteousness extensively. But I feel we have neglected justice as a critical part of any conversation about following the way of the Lord. Look at the last part of Gen. 18:19. Though Abraham has done some amazing things, what are God's promises to Abraham contingent upon? According to this bombshell statement, "so that" the Lord may bring to Abraham what He (The Lord) has promised him (Abraham). Everything that is promised to Abraham flowed from his communicating the Lord's way, righteousness and justice to his children and household.

What will you teach your children and household? Household represents any and all things that are a part of your sphere of influence. My last question, maybe. Do you understand justice well enough to teach it? What if every promise made to you was contingent upon your ability to effectively transfer righteousness and justice to those in your care? That's simply a rhetorical question meant for you to ponder.

There is one other prominent figure from the Old Testament that has a carryover into the New Testament; King David, Solomon's father. David was said to be a man after God's own heart. But more was said about him than that. The New Testament records in Hebrews 11 a list of great people of faith. David is named among several others.

> [32] *"And what more shall I say? For time would fail me to tell of Gideon, Barak, Samson, Jephthah, of David and Samuel and the prophets —* [33] *who through faith conquered kingdoms, enforced justice, obtained promises, stopped the mouths of lions."*
>
> *- Hebrews 11:32-33 (ESV)*

This list of some of the greatest personalities of the Old Testament had some things common to all.

1. They conquered kingdoms. That's a pretty amazing thing.
2. They enforced justice.
3. They obtained promises.

These were promises given to them by God himself. I would say that is pretty spectacular. Then we come to number four of their feat: they "stopped the mouths of lions." I don't know about you, but I think taking on a lion is in the awesome category.

Let's discuss in detail the second description that is nestled in the midst of these astonishing feats; "justice enforcer." Being a justice enforcer according to this writer is on the same level as conquering a kingdom or taking on a lion and winning.

HAVE WE OVERLOOKED THE POWER AND NEED FOR JUSTICE?

David along with tremendous champions of faith were in this list. But I want to continue my focus on David, if I can have your permission? Thank you.

David's early life was spent as a shepherd boy tending sheep. Through a whirlwind of events he became a tremendous King, who conquered many kingdoms. He never lost a battle. He even defeated a giant in battle when he was only a teenager. As king, he built a kingdom that was unrivaled during the time of his reign. David also had some of the fiercest, most loyal, and skilled fighters ever assembled. Many came from far and wide to join David. Some who had been mighty leaders themselves brought all their people, joined David, and submitted themselves and their people to his leadership. What was so different about this leader? What caused his effectiveness? Why would others want to be a part of what this shepherd boy was doing? Take a look at what is said about his way of ruling as a king.

> [15] *"So David reigned over all Israel. And David administered justice and equity to all his people."*
>
> *- 2 Samuel 8:15 (ESV)*

This great king had a "way" he operated. He administered justice and equity. Notice what is considered first, justice. David understood that justice was a necessary dimension of great leadership. He administered it to all his people. Justice was not just for the poor, but for all! When all get justice then all can be just. I indicated David had a New and Old Testament influence. I want to share a couple of other scriptures that shine an even brighter light on this link, but let me give you a little more on this guy David.

David changed everything in the Old Testament. He was a sensitive warrior. What do I mean by that? He was a brilliant strategist in war and fought giants, but he also played musical instruments and wrote some of the most poetic poems ever recorded. He could share the tenderness of his heart with his fiercest fighters and be ruthlessly rigid to those who violated proper decorum for the time. This warrior king, was known by God as "a man after his own heart." Many have said David pursued the heart of God. I want to give you a different perspective. I believe David set as an aspiration to have the same heart as God. God was a God of justice. David administered justice to all His people and wrote in his poetry some of the most profound statements about justice. Take a look.

> [1] *"Give the king your justice, O God,*
> *and your righteousness to the royal son!*
> [2] *May he judge your people with righteousness,*
> *and your poor with justice!"*
>
> *- Psalm 72:1-2 (ESV)*

David understood the justice God delivered to him was his opportunity to have the same heart to others, justice. Let's look at another of his statements on justice.

> [2] **"Who can** *utter the mighty deeds of the LORD,*
> *or declare all his praise?* [3] *Blessed are they who*
> *observe justice, who do righteousness at all times!"*
>
> *- Psalm 106:2-3 (ESV)*

It's amazing the level of value this king, "desiring to have a heart of God to others," places on justice. His statement from verse two "who can," shows there is a limited, exclusive, isolated group who can speak of the mighty deeds of God and who have the ability to declare God's praise. I want you to get what David is saying. If there is anyone who is going to be able to exalt and praise God, this next thing He mentions is the key to bringing God exalted praise. What's next? "Blessed are they who observe justice." I submit for your consideration, doing justice on the earth is the highest praise and exaltation you can give to God! To give love means you are invested in the person and it can be selfish. To give justice you have to operate with the heart of God regardless of your feelings. If we give praise but don't do justice, then our praise is meaningless, because the God of justice is not impressed!

> [3] *"To do righteousness and justice is more acceptable to the LORD than sacrifice."*
>
> *- Proverbs 21:3 (ESV)*

> [6] *"For to us a child is born, to us a son is given; and the government shall be upon his shoulder, and his name shall be called Wonderful Counselor, Mighty God, Everlasting Father, Prince of Peace.* [7] *Of the increase of his government and of peace there will be no end, on the throne of David and over his kingdom, to* **establish** *it and to uphold it with justice and with righteousness from this time forth and forevermore. The zeal of the LORD of hosts will do this."*
>
> *- Isaiah 9:6-7 (ESV)*

Verse seven reveals there is an "increasing government" coming in the future with specific characteristics. There is way too much here to cover it all in this forum. However, I do want to highlight there would be no end to this government once it arrives. Then it is clearly stated, the government would be "on the throne of David and over his kingdom." David's kingdom is identified as the example of how this government will be set up. Now, look at what this kingdom will be established and upheld with: "justice and righteousness." Once this government, kingdom gets underway it will continue forever. Let me make this clear, according to this scripture, justice and righteousness have no shelf life.

If "justice and righteousness" is what the Mighty God is establishing and upholding everything with? Then shouldn't it be our endeavor to understand any concept so powerful it establishes and upholds all God does?

The increase of the government established and upheld by justice and righteousness is the responsibility of the shoulders. Let me now connect David.

When the government, "the shoulder people" (that's you and me on the earth), use the same techniques David used when he was on the throne, when he was advancing his kingdom, we get David results.

Justice and righteousness establish and upholds any endeavor of any people. David was a man of justice. This Mighty God is a God of justice. The government was established and upheld with justice. Once the governments started, from that time forward and throughout eternity justice was to continue. Jesus brought the government back to the earth.

> [17] "From that time Jesus began to preach, saying, "Repent, for the kingdom of heaven is at hand."
>
> - Matthew 4:17 (ESV)

Where do we fit into the equation? A God of justice deserves a people willing to do justice.

> [5] "It is well with the man who deals generously and lends; who conducts his affairs with justice."
>
> - Psalm 112:5 (ESV)

Reader, please hear me. Justice is a part of the fabric of any government's success, even self-government. Justice can establish and uphold anything submitted to it. I will in no way promote or push justice as the end all answer. But I also will not shy away from saying what the scriptures say extensively about justice.

Let's continue with the David connection to justice.

> *³ "Give counsel; grant justice; make your shade like night at the height of noon; shelter the outcasts; do not reveal the fugitive; ⁴ let the outcasts of Moab sojourn among you; be a shelter to them from the destroyer. When the oppressor is no more, and destruction has ceased, and he who tramples underfoot has vanished from the land, ⁵ then a throne will be established in steadfast love, and on it will sit in faithfulness, in the tent of David, one who judges and seeks justice and is swift to do righteousness."*
>
> *- Isaiah 16:3-5 (ESV)*

Here is the David connection. When justice is granted in the way described in verses three and four, then verse five occurs; "then a throne will be established in steadfast love, and on it will sit in faithfulness, in the tent of David, one who judges and seeks justice and is swift to do righteousness."

Here we have the mention of the throne of David again. A throne represents rule, authority, influence and dominion. When we seek justice in our place of rule, authority, influence, and dominion, we reinforce a throne much like that of David, who ruled over his people with justice and equity.

Did you notice the love connection to justice?

WHEN JUSTICE HAS BEEN GRANTED, A THRONE OF STEADFAST LOVE WILL BE ESTABLISHED.

Justice invited and demonstrated what brought about love. The seeker of justice gets to sit on the love throne they created. Justice actions build a throne of love.

Ready to go a little further?

> [5] *"Behold, the days are coming, declares the LORD,
> when I will raise up for David a righteous Branch,
> and he shall reign as king and deal wisely, and shall
> **execute** justice and righteousness in the land."*
>
> *- Jeremiah 23:5*

This scripture speaks of a time to come, when God will raise up for David a righteous Branch (Jesus), and He shall reign as a king and deal wisely. Here is the number one assignment this wise King will implement...execution of justice and righteousness in the land. Jesus from the lineage of David shows up on the scene and operates just as David. He executes justice and righteousness. The very same information is shared in Jeremiah 33:15. Let's cover one last scripture highlighting the David connection before we move on.

> [3] *"Thus says the LORD: Do justice and
> righteousness, and deliver from the hand of the
> oppressor him who has been robbed. And do
> no wrong or violence to the resident alien, the
> fatherless, and the widow, nor shed innocent blood
> in this place. [4] For if you will indeed obey this word,
> then there shall enter the gates of this house kings
> who sit on the throne of David, riding in chariots and
> on horses, they and their servants and their people."*
>
> *- Jeremiah 22:3-4 (ESV)*

What an instruction! It tells us to do justice and righteousness, then tells us exactly *what it looks like* through the rest of verse three. I could spend two chapters on each of the identified recipients, why they are the focus group, and what they represent. "However, for our current purposes, I want to focus on what happens in our lives, cities, territories, and countries when we do justice as described.

Verse four says, if you obey "this word." What word? "Do justice and righteousness!" "Then shall enter the gates of this house."

"This house" represents the same instruction delivered to Abraham concerning his children and household. Whatever and wherever you have influence and authority gets the promised benefit. What was unique about the throne/rule of David?

THE WAY OF JUSTICE

> [15] *"David reigned over all Israel*
> *with justice and equity."*
>
> *- 2 Samuel 8:15*

David had a way he operated and became a great king who was unparalleled. Justice was his key! But the last part of verse four is the tremendous two-part takeaway. Part one: when a just ruler is operating, it produces a notable position represented by chariots and horses, which were considered symbols of the most prominently esteemed individuals.

The takeaway part two comes next. The prominence of the justice ruler is transferred to all who are with him (servants and people)! Justice is transferable! Justice is contagious. Justice releases the champion in those around you and in your care! Justice takes your authority to the epic proportions of David's rule!

CHAPTER FOUR
ANYWHERE, REALLY?

> [4] *"The King in his might loves justice. You have established equity; you have executed justice and righteousness in Jacob."*
>
> *- Psalm 99:4*

David was a tremendous leader who administered justice and equity! People in leadership who do not recognize their might (strength, effectiveness, ability, capability, wisdom, insight, and leadership) flows out of a love for justice, will soon sabotage the position they hold. In Psalm 99:4 the scripture says this person has "established equity." Here's what equity entails: freedom from bias or favoritism. Leaders will not be effective without ensuring those they lead, whether they like them or not, get an unbiased assessment.

A true leader sets equity as a foundation for leading, established (past tense) equity. They don't wait until a circumstance arises and then try to come up with the appropriate principle. Equity opens the door for you to execute justice and righteousness. You can't do justice and righteousness justly without equity being a prerequisite.

"In Jacob" means this affected all people as Jacob represented the entirety of the Jewish people. When leaders put in place that which provides opportunity for friend, foe, family, favorite, frivolous, and fool to be handled in a just way, then cultures, cities, neighborhoods, homes, and individuals can be transformed. Equity is an invitation to participate in the eradication of injustice! Let's take a look at some scriptures that support leadership.

> [1] *"Run to and fro through the streets of Jerusalem, look and take note! Search her squares to see if you can find a man, one who does justice and seeks truth, that I may pardon her."*
>
> *- Jeremiah 5:1 (ESV)*

THE WAY OF JUSTICE

Jerusalem is representative of any city anywhere in the world. The writer says in any city anywhere in the world we are to be searching for someone specific to take note of this unique person. What person are we seeking? One who does justice and seeks truth. Let me reveal a secret. These individuals are any city's true leaders. What is the result of the actions of this type person? The city is pardoned! What an interesting word to use. Pardon means to excuse, release, remove penalty, release from punishment, and to take away the offence. Justice is the key to reclaiming, restoring, and redeeming our cities.

Many cities across the U.S. and throughout the world have corruption, violence, murders, poverty, briberies, deception, injustice and oppression. Those things being in our cities is not what's noteworthy. When we find those, who do justice and seek truth, they become those to take note of. Being able to find those who do justice and seek truth can neutralize any city's shortcomings. They are the ones we should follow. They are the ones we should model. They are the ones who will right the wrongs in cities by using their capabilities and means willingly.

According to this scripture God pays attention to these people. It is because of these justice doers and truth seekers, God pardons. Can I invite you to consider something at this juncture? Could it be God is waiting to find those who can be trusted to do justice so He can bring justice to the earth, to your city? While we are here in Jeremiah 5, let's look at what's said in verses four and five.

> [4] "Then I said, "These are only the poor;
> they have no sense; for they do not know the
> **way** of the LORD, the justice of their God."
>
> - Jeremiah 5:4 (ESV)

As the searcher of the streets is looking for the doer of justice that seeks truth, the search runs across a group of people or should I say a type of people. They are called "only the poor." They are said to have no sense. Why? "For they do not know the way of the Lord, the justice of their God"! My God, what a powerful indictment. I want to point out here that the "way of the Lord" and "justice" are used as synonymous terms. I also want to point out here that poor has nothing to do with economics, but with not knowing justice, the way of the Lord. I will let that simmer for a moment while we go on to verse five.

> [5] *"I will go to the great and will speak to them, for they know the way of the LORD, the justice of their God." But they all alike had broken the yoke; they had burst the bonds."*
>
> *- Jeremiah 5:5 (ESV)*

As the person continues through the streets of the city, he encounters another group called the great. So the searcher of the streets has found two types of people, **poor type and a great type**. The poor type has not heard of justice and the need for it. But this other group, the great group, seems to have been taught or at least at some time in the past, been exposed to justice and the fact it was the way of the Lord. However, there is a problem. They had broken the yoke and burst the bonds. Let's put that in layman's terms. They knew what they should be doing, but are now choosing not to follow through.

If I may, many of our politicians run campaigns promising justice, equity, righteousness, fairness, care and change for the good. However, shortly after getting in office they seem to break the yoke of their promises, they burst the bonds of their seemingly strong convictions they espoused during their campaigning. They were proclaiming a message when we initially found them in the streets, but now their actions no longer resemble what was originally found in their proclamations. They advocated for social justice and gave us legalized extortion. They touted protecting rights, but violate any not meeting their cause/sacred group's identity. They deliver a so-called justice hollow of truth, equity, objective measure, or compassion. They ripped the heart out of justice.

A yoke is a responsibility *towards* a thing. A bond is that which *guarantees* a thing. We must return to being responsible and fulfilling the guarantees we once knew and promised. Poor and great is not the issue. The poor can learn justice. The great can return to justice before they become poor again, by not continuing in the way of the Lord they once knew. But both have to recognize justice is what will bring the pardoning of God to their city and streets. Three types of people emerge from these passages. Those who don't know justice, those who know it and don't do it, and those who know and do justice as the way of the Lord. Which will help your city?

True social justice warriors on the streets of our cities are to be commended. But I caution them to remain just and not allow their yokes to be broken and their bonds to burst. Execute true justice that is not a watered-down attempt at notoriety. There are those who espouse justice, but do they seek truth? Truth is a key component. True justice will always seek truth in a neutral way. Neutral means no predetermined outcomes. Truth is allowed regardless of benefit to the person seeking it. Truth is not personal and carries no personal pronouns. It is a definite article, the truth in spite of and regardless of the individual. Return to truth. Return to justice. Stay with truth. Stay with justice. Your city is depending on you. Others are looking for you. God has a written pardon in his hand waiting for you to be found. One last thought before we go on. There are rights we all have. However, a basic human right does not establish a right to use unjust means to meet those rights!

> [1] *"And I said: Hear, you heads of Jacob and rulers of the house of Israel! Is it not for you to know justice?"*
>
> *- Micah 3:1 (ESV)*

I say to the readers of these pages, is it not for you to know justice?

Abraham, Solomon, and David who were three of the most renowned individuals in the Old and New Testaments. Each had justice as a foundation of their lives. They sought justice, embraced justice, executed justice, administered justice, and enforced justice! They each understood the God of justice, expected justice from those who would be used by him. Each of these men have been heralded as examples of faith, leadership, conviction, wisdom, and strength. The common denominator for all these guys was justice. Justice is a mark of great leaders!

WISE LEADERS EXECUTE JUSTICE IN THE LAND WHERE THEY HAVE INFLUENCE.

If we have any place of leadership, any place of influence, any place of authority; are we seeking and executing justice? "By justice a king (leader) builds up the land, but he that exacts taxes tears it down" Proverbs 29:4. A leader uses justice to build those in his territory. What is your territory? What are you to be building?

Solomon, Abraham, and David are tremendous examples because they represent us. They show us we can be people of justice. I want to highlight one last individual who understood the need for justice. He came as the last Adam.

> [18] "Behold, my servant whom I have chosen, my beloved with whom my soul is well pleased. I will put my Spirit upon him, and he will proclaim justice to the Gentiles. [19] He will not quarrel or cry aloud, nor will anyone hear his voice in the streets; [20] a bruised reed he will not break, and a smoldering wick he will not quench, until he brings justice to victory; [21] and in his name the Gentiles will hope."
>
> - Matthew 12:18-21 (ESV)

This passage is of course speaking of Jesus. He came that we might have life and have it more abundantly. He became poor that we might become rich. He humbled Himself that we might be exalted. We received redemption because He was condemned. He became sin to remove our sin. He came in the flesh as a son to restore all mankind to our relationship with the Father of creation. I could go on for the next ten chapters of why Jesus became for us. However, let's unfold the passage above.

In Matthew 12:18-21, Jesus is quoting from Isaiah 42:1-4 about Himself. If you refer back to the passage referenced, then you discover it can apply to any person, namely the one who embraces it as truth for them.

The first word in Matthew 12:18 is "behold." That means pay attention. Give notice to this. Remember our scripture from Jeremiah 5:1, "run to and fro throughout the streets of Jerusalem, look and take note."

THE WAY OF JUSTICE

As we can see from the text, this servant is *chosen* and *pleases* God the Father. God then promises to put His Spirit upon Him, this chosen servant with whom God is well pleased. Why? What is the reason? What happens after this chosen One has the Spirit? "He will proclaim justice to the Gentiles;" that's us, any non-Jewish person.

Verse nineteen is amazing because it indicates the singular focus of God's servant Jesus. He won't be quarreling, arguing and disputing in the streets about meaningless things. His demeanor will be one that builds and doesn't break. He fans the flames of life and doesn't quench them. His unwavering focus is narrowed to one thing, "until He brings justice to victory." These few verses unveil a God-sized assignment; bringing justice to victory! The last verse tells what can and will bring the assignment to fruition. In His name, the Gentiles (we) will hope. We are His shoulders, His body. His justice victory comes through us. Jesus will work in, through, and with each of us who's willing to use his or her capability and means to bring justice to victory!

I have been in the Lord for over thirty years. I have never heard this last statement identified as much more than a feel-good proclamation about victory. But justice was not in the least expressed as essential in any discussion I've had. But with what we have learned to this point, I feel justice is the focus of what our Lord is looking to bring to the earth, cities, homes, and individuals. Justice brings victory. Justice is the key to victory. Justice takes those who have been bruised, those whose flame is flickering and brings them back to a place of victory. When life has slapped any of us down with circumstance beyond our control, what can help us have a comeback? I suggest to you this passage provides hope. I believe

JESUS CAN AND WILL GIVE US VICTORY THROUGH JUSTICE.

Jesus' justice to us and our justice to others is a God formula for victorious comebacks!

Now I want you to insert yourself into Matthew 12:18-21. God is talking to you the person who has been devastated and reading this booklet. ¹⁸ "Behold, my servant (____Your Name____) whom I have chosen, my beloved (____Your Name____) with whom my soul is well pleased. I will put my Spirit upon him/her (____Your Name____), and he/she (____Your Name____) will proclaim (live) justice to the Gentiles. ¹⁹ He/she (____Your Name____) will not quarrel or cry aloud, nor will anyone hear his/her (____Your Name____) voice in the streets; ²⁰ a bruised reed he/her (____Your Name____) will not break, and a smoldering wick he/she (____Your Name____) will not quench, until he/she (____Your Name____) brings justice to victory; ²¹ and in his/her name (____Your Name____) the Gentiles (people of the world) will hope."

When you are that type of model for justice, you bring hope to others. Others learn the right way of living. Their lives can become smooth again. Your life can come back to being a level platform to launch any endeavor of the Lord. You become "others focused" which centers God's focus on you! The way to God is focusing on others. And the King will answer them:

> ⁴⁰ "Truly, I say to you, as you did it to one of the
> least of these my brothers, you did it to me."
> - Matthew 25:40 (ESV)

In chapter 1 of this booklet, I referenced Isaiah 26 which says, *"my soul longs to be with you at night and my spirit yearns to be with you at the dawn of every day, for when your way of justice comes to the land the world will learn the right way of living."*

How will Jesus bring justice to victory? By bringing each of us to victory. Justice brings victory for those who will embrace a justice mandate in the face of tremendous odds. Your life becomes the bruised reed Jesus uses. Your flickering flame becomes the igniter for a blaze in someone's darkness. Victory is promised and possible, but justice is the key component. God says, behold my servant who I uphold (lift, exalt, use, supply, sustain, undergird, promote, and make a light to others)! I truly feel if you have taken time to read this book and you have made it this far, you are the one your God is talking to and looking for. You are the servant He beholds!

THE WAY OF JUSTICE

I am in real estate. Something interestingly revealing happened while on a listing appointment with my client (a person considering/preparing to sell his property). I had known my client for ten years, and as we were catching up, he told me a story of how he is being relocated to the town where he and his wife have always wanted to retire. This man is now an executive in his organization. But he started from the bottom. He told me the transfer he is getting doesn't normally happen, however, one of the senior vice presidents had made it happen for him. Here was the amazing thing; the guy who was the senior vice president, his boss's boss, used to work for this gentleman. He recalled meeting the young man about the time he had purchased his home some ten years earlier. The young man was headstrong and didn't understand the essence of being faithful and doing your best even if you didn't plan to stay with a company. As he continued, he told of how he took him under his wing and helped him learn. Ten years later the same guy he helped be a better employee has far surpassed him. This same guy orchestrated the move!

When we willing use our capability and mean to put things right for others in a just way, they learn the right way of living and become effective. The path of life for both of these individuals is level and smooth. This young man simply needed guidance to become. When we are that guidance for other with our justice, things can be transformed for many around us. The gentleman I was discussing this with wasn't a king, but he was a leader and had influence which he used to put things right.

> [9] "The **humble** He **guides** with justice,
> the humble he **teaches** His **way**."
>
> - Psalm 25:9 (NKJV)

This is a Psalm where God Himself is saying who He will assist in being effective. The humble are those who have a proper estimation of themselves, no more and no less. These individuals get God's attention. If you will, these are the individuals who qualify for God's assistance. When God finds any such person,

"He guides [them] with justice." God guides them to use their capability and means to willingly put things right for others. Guides means to walk with, lead, to tread down a path, to show, and to bend. The bend is like shooting an arrow with accuracy or calibrating to fit.

There is a path, a way of justice that the humble are taught. The last part of the verse shows us the "way of God" is the way of justice. Both parts of the verse are saying the exact same thing.

His name was Ashed, he was an immigrant from Turkey who had lived in Dallas, Texas for three years. He was the Uber driver I used to travel from my hotel to the airport. I was in Dallas for a veteran's fundraising event. Ashed had been a refugee in Turkey for several years, but he had grown up in a war-torn part of Pakistan. His wife had been the executive secretary of one of the ministers in the government of Pakistan. He had gone to school to be a dentist and had built a great practice. They were considered well off by all standards in their country, but he realized they had arrived at the pinnacle of where their lives would reach. I asked what he meant by the statement.

"In my country, there are no aspirations to get or do better," he said. "If the stars align and you can get an education and arrive at a level of success, you consider yourself fortunate...but that usually is the sum total of what life will be from that time. There is no incentive or reward for doing more, If you do, then it just goes to the government."

When the fighting got so severe, he and his wife had to flee their homeland, and they ended up in Turkey as refugees. The problem was for over four years they were not allowed to work. They had to be totally dependent on the Turkish government for food, housing, medical care and any other necessity. For Ashed and his wife, it was humiliating and demoralizing. It was during this time Ashed and his wife decided if they ever had the opportunity again, they would help others never have to depend on handouts. They were accepted into a program to migrate to the U.S., they got green cards, and they began working again.

When they arrived in the U.S., they were given an apartment in Dallas, food vouchers, eight hundred dollars per month, and a work permit. Ashed stunned me with what he said next.

"We only took the vouchers and funds for four months," he said. "By then, I was working two jobs and a third one part time. My wife

THE WAY OF JUSTICE

was also working two jobs. We quickly saw that here in the U.S. if you worked, then you were able to keep the fruit of your labor. We determined the only thing that can keep us from being successful here is us."

When they heard about the Uber boom in cities around the country, they came up with a plan to put enough money away to buy a car that met at least the minimum requirements to be an Uber approved vehicle.

"Is this the vehicle," I asked?

"No," he replied. "We have recently upgraded to this one, so we can carry more high-end clients." Ashed, then told me the next shocker, he and his wife have worked seven days a week for the last three years. They now have a limousine service and drive for Uber and Lift. And they are buying their first house at a cost of $350,000.

"It is under contract," he said. "We close next week, and it is beautiful. My wife loves the counter tops."

I asked, "how long did you say you have been in the U.S.?"

"Only three years," he replied. I then asked how he and his wife accomplished this so quickly.

He told me he and his wife went through a program by Dave Ramsey on being debt free and having financial freedom. He said, he and his wife wanted to be able to help others, but couldn't if all their funds were going to sustain them. The next shocker he said was, "the only debt we will have will be our new home, which we plan to pay off as soon as possible."

This man became my hero sitting right there in his Uber. Then he said something that made the entire drive worth the price and then some.

"I use my Uber to share my story with others," he said. "Sometimes I don't charge depending on how I feel about where the person is in life. I tell others, 'if I as an immigrant here in a foreign country can make it, then anyone can'."

Boy did I give Ashed a great tip. My entire trip to Dallas was worth that Uber ride. By the way, Ashed and his wife were helping others get into business also to give back in response to all they had received. Ashed and his wife were using their capability and means to put things right for others. Without knowing it, they were doing acts of justice. Now back to our text and the way of justice.

Just so you don't think I am pushing what is not here in the scripture, let's take a look at what another writer had to say.

> [4] "The Rock, his work is perfect, for all his **ways** are justice. A God of faithfulness and without iniquity, just and upright is he."
>
> - Deuteronomy 32:4 (ESV)

All His ways are justice! If His ways are justice and we are created in His image, wouldn't it stand to reason our ways should be justice also? But I get it, this is God, we can't expect to operate as He does, or should we? Not unless that is exactly what he says for us to do. I will do this next scripture out of order for effect, but you will get the point. "Justice, and only justice, you shall follow, that you may live and inherit the land that the LORD your God is giving you."

That is pretty clear isn't it? I thought so, too. I discovered justice has application in everything we do. Whether it is being a husband, wife, father, mother, sister, brother, friend, worker, supervisor, athlete or you just interact with others in life. Justice is a societal need if our interactions are to be fruitful and healthy. Justice doesn't guarantee fairness; it just guarantees the right principles of fairness are used in our interactions with life. Justice governs our interaction with others if we allow it. Justice ensures our interactions are just.

"THERE IS NO VIRTUE SO TRULY GREAT AND GODLIKE AS JUSTICE" - ENGLISH POET JOSEPH ADDISON

Now, we can take a look at the first parts of the passage.

THE WAY OF JUSTICE

> [18] "You shall appoint judges and officers in all your towns that the LORD your God is giving you, according to your tribes, and they shall judge the people with righteous judgment. [19] You shall not pervert justice. You shall not show partiality, and you shall not accept a bribe, for a bribe blinds the eyes of the wise and subverts the cause of the righteous."
>
> - Deuteronomy 16:18-19 (ESV)

The writer of this passage understood no matter where these people resided, there had to be the establishment of order, in order for the place they occupied to have success. They are encouraged to not pervert justice with one another. How is justice perverted? Showing partiality, that's when we make decisions based on anything other than doing right by others as a person. Accepting a bribe is taking advantage of a situation with gain to you as the motivation; it's considered unacceptable. A bribe blinds the eyes of the otherwise wise and subverts (undermines, distorts, dismantles) the person who is right. If a person is right regardless of your feelings, benefit to you, or whether you have good feeling toward them, they are still right and must be treated as such. Justice ensure equitable treatment for friend and foe.

> [25] "There is a way that seems right to a person, but its end is death."
>
> - Proverbs 16:25

When we withhold, refuse, neglect, and pervert justice we bring death to what should be life. Without justice we kill what we intend to create. Until justice is a core part of our being as an unshakable value; we are susceptible to unjust acts at any time. The justice way! It is a path less traveled, because most have not the courage, heart, or knowledge of the way.

> [4] "Give attention to me my people, give ear to me my nation, for a law will go out from me and I will set justice as a light to the people."
> (nations & people groups)
>
> - Isaiah 51:4

CHAPTER FIVE
"THE WAY"

It was a Sunday morning when I saw Misha. I didn't know that was her name. All I knew was as I drove to church, I saw a lady walking barefoot on the road. I stopped to see if I could assist and immediately noticed swollen eyes red from crying and tattered hair. The lady asked if I could drive her about ten minutes away to a friend's home. She had no purse, she didn't have on a jacket and it was cold outside, so I agreed.

I didn't want to pry so I remained quiet, only asking for directions as we went along. She finally broke the silence.

"Thank you so much for stopping for me," she said. "My husband and I had a terrible fight and I had to leave because he had become violent."

At that point she began to cry. When we pulled up in front of the friend's house, she again said thank you and indicated she could go borrow some money from the friend to pay me. I told her it truly was not a problem and she didn't owe me a dime. Right in that moment I can't even say why I did it, but I said, "ma'am, today is a difficult day and your world is in turmoil, but you will laugh again and what you feel today will be turned into joy. God will ensure it."

Tears streamed down her face again as she departed my vehicle.

Eight years later, I heard my name being called.

"You are Steffron, aren't you?"

I turned to see a lady walking towards me. I'm in real estate and have no idea at times who I have met and when, so I figured it was someone from a previous transaction.

THE WAY OF JUSTICE

"You probably don't know my name or who I am do you," the lady asked. I learned long ago not to try to play it off like you remember a person if you don't. So I said, "no ma'am, I don't. Could you refresh my memory?"

"My name is Misha," she said. "You picked me up over eight years ago walking barefoot on a Sunday morning, you were on the way to church and dropped me off at a friend's house."

It all came flooding back to me.

"Oh yes! It is great to see you again," I said. Then it came. The part that brought me to tears right there standing in a parking lot.

She said, "not a day has gone by in the last eight years that I have not thanked God for you. The words you spoke to me before I got out of your car have carried me. There were more dark times; I ended up getting a divorce. But now I am married to a wonderful man and I am laughing again. My life was in shambles that morning, but something about your words has led me to where I am today. My life looks nothing like it did and I trace it all back to that Sunday morning."

We hugged, wished each other the best and turned to continue our day. But as I walked away, I couldn't help but recall, I almost didn't stop because I didn't want to be late for church.

Justice will provide a light that illuminates a way for God's people, any people to walk. The way of justice is the way of life! However, we must take the initiative to learn the way of justice. We must learn to do good and seek justice opportunities Isaiah 1:17. As we bring this to a close, please hear well these last two verses.

> [5] *"Evil men do not understand justice, but those who seek the Lord understand it completely."*
>
> *- Proverbs 28:5*

The indictment of this verse is that if you don't understand justice, then there is a propensity to evil, because you have no idea when you violate a justice principle. But if you are seeking the Lord, you can't help but find and grasp justice completely, because God is a God of justice. Our last scripture is a promise for those who go this way called justice.

> [20] *"I walk in the way of righteousness, in the paths (ways) of justice,* [21] *granting an inheritance to those who love me, and filling their treasuries."*
>
> *- Proverbs 8:20-21 (ESV)*

There is a way! There is a path! Treasures are there and it is a part of your inheritance. On what path will you be found?

JUSTICE IS THE WAY, WALK IN IT!

THE WAY OF JUSTICE

Thank you for taking this journey with me;
for together, we are indeed

CHAMPIONS OF JUSTICE!

ABOUT THE AUTHOR
STEFFRON T. JAMES

Steffron T. James is a South Carolina native. He has made Tennessee his home for the past 17 years. He fondly refers to Tennessee as "the place where God lives." He served our country 22 1/2 years in the US Air Force. He enjoys real estate as his fun day job. Business development and entrepreneurship intrigue him, and he loves teaching and applying sound business practices in various aspects of life. Steffron's greatest passion is teaching the Word of God while challenging individuals to personal development and aspiring to their fullest potential. He is the author of Champions of Justice, the companion book to this one. His five children, three grandchildren, and a multitude of spiritual sons and daughters keep him young and enjoying life.

For more information visit: *www.thewayofjustice.com*

JUSTICE SERIES - VOL 1

THE CAUSE OF JUSTICE

BRINGING JUSTICE TO YOUR CAUSE

Available at *www.thewayofjustice.com*

JUSTICE SERIES – VOL 2

STREETS OF JUSTICE

RETURNING TRUTH TO THE PUBLIC SQUARE

Available at *www.thewayofjustice.com*

JUSTICE SERIES - VOL 3

THE PATH OF JUSTICE

TAPPING INTO YOUR TREASURES!

Available at *www.thewayofjustice.com*

CHAMPIONS OF JUSTICE
DIVINE EMPOWERMENT FOR WEALTH

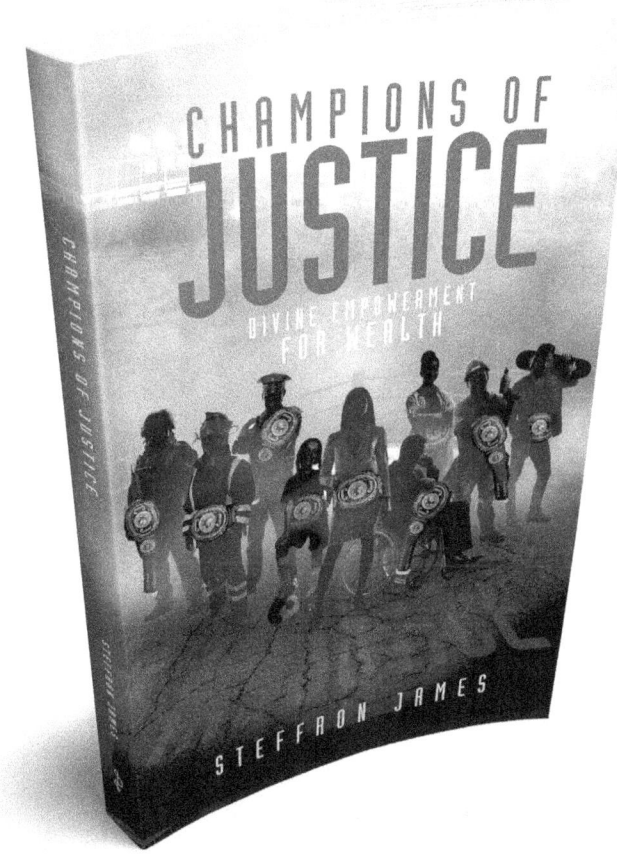

Available at *www.thewayofjustice.com*

JUSTICE SERIES - VOL 4

THE WAY OF JUSTICE

THE GAME CHANGER

STEFFRON T. JAMES

Copyright © 2020 by The Way of Justice - All Rights Reserved.

www.ingramcontent.com/pod-product-compliance
Lightning Source LLC
Chambersburg PA
CBHW032217040426
42449CB00005B/647